My Favorite Horse

Appaloosas Are My Favorite!

Elaine Landau

LERNER PUBLICATIONS COMPANY • MINNEAPOLIS

Copyright © 2012 by Lerner Publishing Group, Inc.

All rights reserved. International copyright secured. No part of this book may be reproduced, stored in a retrieval system, or transmitted in any form or by any means—electronic, mechanical, photocopying, recording, or otherwise—without the prior written permission of Lerner Publishing Group, Inc., except for the inclusion of brief quotations in an acknowledged review.

Lerner Publications Company
A division of Lerner Publishing Group, Inc.
241 First Avenue North
Minneapolis, MN 55401 U.S.A.

Website address: www.lernerbooks.com

Library of Congress Cataloging-in-Publication Data

Landau, Elaine.
  Appaloosas are my favorite! / by Elaine Landau.
    p. cm. — (My favorite horses)
  Includes index.
  ISBN 978-0-7613-6535-8 (lib. bdg. : alk. paper)
  1. Appaloosa horse—Juvenile literature. I. Title.
SF293.A7L36 2012
  636.1'3—dc22   2011011663

Manufactured in the United States of America
1 – PP – 12/31/11

PHOTO ACKNOWLEDGMENTS

The images in this book are used with the permission of: © Darlene Wohlart, pp. 2, 4, 6, 7, 8, 15, 16, 19, 20; © SportAction/Alamy, p. 9; © bojangles/Alamy, pp. 10–11; National Anthropological Archives, Smithsonian Institution/NAA INV 06479800, p. 12; University of Washington Libraries, Special Collections, NA975, p. 13; © SuperStock, p. 14; © Lynn Stone/AgStock Images/Corbis/CORBIS, p. 17; © Barbara O'Brien Photography, p. 18; © Jutta Klee/CORBIS, p. 21; © Mark J. Barrett/www.kimballstock.com, p. 22.

Front Cover: © Adam Goss/Dreamstime.com.
Back Cover: © Isselee/Dreamstime.com.

Main body text set in Atelier Sans ITC Std 16/24.
Typeface provided by International Typeface Corp.

TABLE OF CONTENTS

Introduction
THERE'S NOTHIN' LIKE A HORSE ... 5

Chapter One
MEET THE APPALOOSA ... 6

Chapter Two
APPALOOSA HISTORY ... 12

Chapter Three
THE REAL DEAL ... 16

Glossary ... 23

For More Information ... 24

Index ... 24

INTRODUCTION
THERE'S NOTHIN' LIKE A HORSE

Question: What's better than traveling by bike or by skateboard?

Answer: Going by horse, of course!

Do you dream of owning a horse? Can you see yourself riding through a lush green meadow? What a great feeling! Bet you know the kind of horse you want. It's an Appaloosa. That's a wonderful breed.

But wait! What about your parents? Have they said yes to a hamster but no to a horse?

So what's a horse-crazy kid to do? You can't pretend that your bike has a mane and a tail forever. Must you forget about ever having a horse?

No way! You can still learn all about the Appaloosa. Besides, you won't always be a kid. Someday you just may own one of these terrific horses.

Chapter One
MEET THE APPALOOSA

The Appaloosa is a beautiful animal. It's known for its striking, spotted coat. The spots often appear on an Appaloosa's back and hips. It looks as if the horse is wearing a spotted blanket. Other Appaloosas have spots all over their bodies. No two horses' spots are the same.

Surprise!
Not all Appaloosas have spots. Some are a solid color. Yet they can still have spotted foals.

Mottled Skin

Appaloosas have mottled skin. *Mottled* means "covered with different patches of color." An Appaloosa's skin is often pink with darker patches.

Jeepers! What a Pair of Peepers!

An Appaloosa's eyes look a lot like a human's eyes. That's because you can see this horse's sclera. The sclera is the white part of the eyes. It doesn't show in most horses.

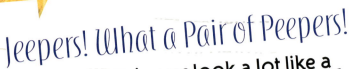

Fancy Feet

Horses don't wear designer shoes. But **Appaloosas** have fancy feet. Their hooves are striped!

Size, Strength, and Smarts

The Appaloosa is about fourteen to fifteen hands tall at the highest part of its back. All horses are measured in hands. One hand is equal to 4 inches (10 centimeters). Appaloosas weigh between 950 and 1,250 pounds (431 and 567 kilograms).

The Appaloosa is both smart and strong. It's also very gentle. These horses are great for young children and new riders. There's a lot to love about Appaloosas.

Horsey Math

This equation shows about how high an Appaloosa is in inches and centimeters.

$$\begin{array}{r} 14 \text{ hands} \\ \times\ 4 \text{ inches (10 cm)} \\ \hline 56 \text{ inches (142 cm)} \end{array}$$

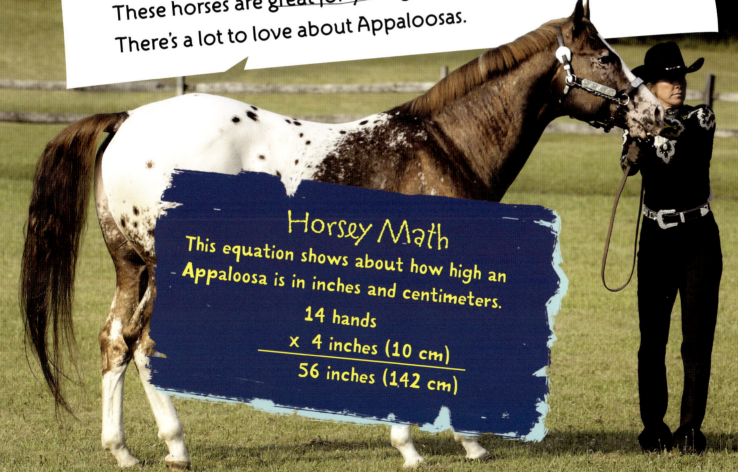

Parts of a Horse

You know that horses have a mane, a tail, and four hooves. But can you find a horse's chestnut? Or its withers? Let's take a closer look at a horse. Soon you'll be an expert on all the parts that make up these magnificent animals.

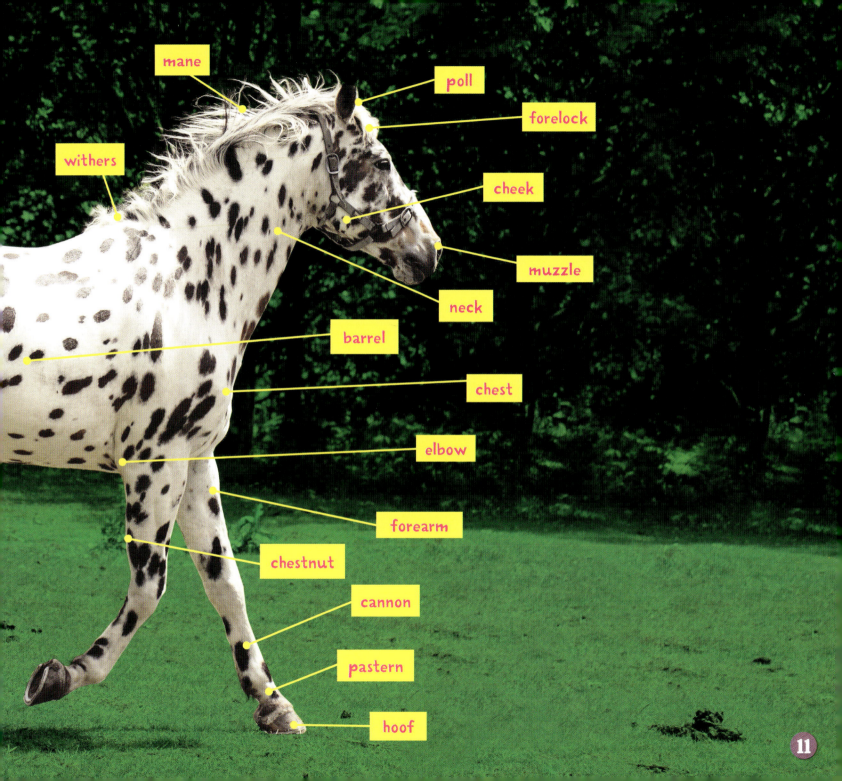

Chapter Two
APPALOOSA HISTORY

Appaloosas aren't new. They're related to North America's earliest horses. Spanish explorers first brought horses to North America in the sixteenth century. By the early 1700s, the Nez Percé Indians were riding them when hunting buffalo.

The Nez Percé bred the fastest, hardiest horses of the bunch. They also chose the most colorful, spotted horses to breed. They ended up with the horse we know as the Appaloosa.

A Nez Percé Indian sits atop a horse.

Hard Times

Appaloosas helped the Nez Percé a great deal. The horses could easily keep up with buffalo herds. But by the late 1800s, Appaloosas were in trouble. Settlers from Europe wanted the Nez Percé's land. War broke out between the Nez Percé and the settlers. The Nez Percé lost. The settlers took most of their horses.

Settlers kept some of the horses for themselves. But they shot many others. It looked as if the Appaloosa might die out.

An Appaloosa stands on grassy land in the early 1900s. The Appaloosa was in danger of dying out at this time.

A New Dawn

But in the 1930s, things improved for Appaloosas. Not many of these horses were left—yet people still praised their beauty and style. In time, more riders wanted to own them. Soon these horses were being bred in greater numbers.

The State Horse

States often have official state flowers, trees, and animals. These symbols help represent the states. Idaho has an official state horse. **Can you guess what it is?** That's right—it's the **Appaloosa!**

Nowadays

These days, the Appaloosa is used for racing and in rodeos. People also like riding it for pleasure. It looks as if this breed is here to stay.

Fast on His Feet

Apache Double was a great racehorse. This **Appaloosa** set fourteen world records for speed. He was also the first **Appaloosa** to win more than $2 million on the racetrack. Apache Double died on October 23, 1999, at the age of thirty. But loyal **Appaloosa** fans still remember him.

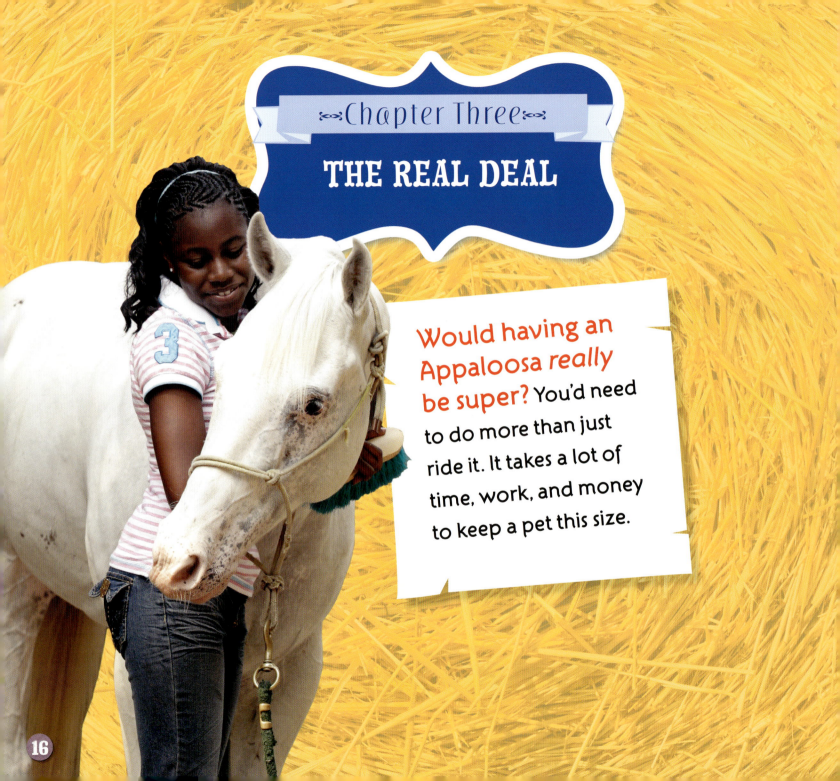

Chapter Three
THE REAL DEAL

Would having an Appaloosa *really* be super? You'd need to do more than just ride it. It takes a lot of time, work, and money to keep a pet this size.

A Home for Your Horse

You can keep a bird or a rabbit in your room. But that won't work with a horse. Does your family live on a large farm? If so, your horse can stay in a fenced-in pasture. Your horse would also need a shelter of some type. This could be a basic three-sided shelter to protect the horse in bad weather or on very hot days.

You'd have to spend lots of time in the pasture too. You'd need to go there to feed and groom your horse. You'd also have to clean up its manure, or droppings. Horses make about 50 pounds (23 kg) of manure daily. Get a big shovel, and roll up your sleeves.

Stable Boarding

You can board your horse at a stable if you don't have very much land. People there can care for the animal. This is called full board. But it's extremely expensive. Many families can't afford it.

Another choice is for you to take care of your own horse at a stable. You'd have to go there every day to feed and groom it. You'd have to shovel the manure out of its stall too.

Taking Care of Tack

Still another job awaits you if you have a horse. Tack is the gear used in horseback riding. It includes the saddle, reins, and other items. Horse owners have to wash their tack weekly.

Riding Styles

There are two main riding styles. One style is called English. The other is called Western. In English riding, riders hold the reins with both hands. They use a lightweight saddle that has a nearly flat seat. In Western riding, riders hold the reins with one hand. They use a saddle that has a high front and back. Western saddles also have a horn.

Both English and Western riding can be done for pleasure or for money or prizes in horse shows. Whichever way you ride, play it safe. Be sure to wear a helmet.

Out of the Gate with Different Gaits

Horses move in different ways. These are known as gaits. Walking is the slowest gait. When a horse is walking, it lifts one foot at a time off the ground. Trotting is the next-fastest gait. Here two of the horse's legs move forward at the same time. A canter is faster than a trot. The canter is a three-beat gait. A gallop is the fastest gait of all. It feels like a fast canter.

Horse Crazy

You don't have to own a horse to enjoy these animals. Try some of these fun horse-related activities instead.

Make horses your hobby.
Look for books, magazines, and DVDs about Appaloosas. Check out YouTube videos about them too. Become an Appaloosa expert!

Create an Appaloosa scrapbook.
Cut out pictures of Appaloosas. Include notes about famous horses of this breed. Choose your favorites.

Get up close.
Many summer camps have horses. The campers ride and help care for the animals. Maybe you can go to one. Or ask your parents if you can take riding lessons. This costs much less than owning a horse. You'll get a chance to ride different horses too.

Appaloosas are really beautiful. It's hard not to fall for them. Maybe you'll get to ride an Appaloosa. Or perhaps you'll just learn more about this breed. One thing is certain: you'll have fun finding out all about these great animals!

GLOSSARY

breed: a particular type of horse. Horses of the same breed have the same body shape and general features. *Breed* can also refer to producing horses.

foal: a young horse

full board: an arrangement in which a horse owner pays staff at a stable to feed and care for the horse

gait: a word to describe a horse's movements. The four gaits are walk, trot, canter, and gallop.

groom: to brush and clean a horse

hand: a unit for measuring horses. One hand is equal to 4 inches (10 cm).

horn: a knob at the front of a Western-style saddle

mottled: covered with different patches of color

sclera: the white part of the eyes

tack: a horse's gear, including its saddle, reins, and bridle

FOR MORE INFORMATION

Brecke, Nicole, and Patricia M. Stockland. *Horses You Can Draw.* Minneapolis: Millbrook Press, 2010. Especially designed for horse lovers, this colorful book shows young readers how to draw different kinds of horses.

Criscione, Rachel Damon. *The Appaloosa.* New York: PowerKids Press, 2007. Find out more about the Appaloosa in this interesting selection.

Horsefun
http://www.horsefun.com
This website is all about kids and horses. You'll find lots of horsey quizzes, puzzles, and games here. The site also features handy hints for young riders.

Landau, Elaine. *Your Pet Pony.* New York: Children's Press, 2007. This is a good guide for young people on what it takes to own and care for a pony.

Linde, Barbara M. *Famous Horses.* New York: Gareth Stevens, 2011. Horse-crazy kids will love reading about famous horses in this fun book.

McDaniel, Lurlene. *A Horse for Mandy.* Minneapolis: Darby Creek, 2004. On her thirteenth birthday, Mandy gets her dream gift—a horse of her own. But will Mandy and her horse be able to save her best friend when tragedy strikes?

LERNER SOURCE
Expand learning beyond the printed book. Download free, complementary educational resources for this book from our website, www.lerneresource.com.

INDEX

color, 7

diagram, 10–11

gaits, 20

history, 12–14

horse ownership, 16–19

riding styles, 19

size, 9